# Olivia Lauren's
## GUIDE TO BECOMING AN ACTOR

Written and Illustrated by

**Olivia Lauren & Melissa-Sue John**

*Lauren Simone Publishing House*

© 2017 LAUREN SIMONE PUBLISHING HOUSE

ALL RIGHTS RESERVED

In accordance with the U.S. Copyright Act of 1976, the scanning, uploading, and electronic sharing of any part of this book without the permission of the publisher constitute unlawful piracy and theft of the author's intellectual property. If you would like to use material from the book (other than for review purposes), prior written permission must be obtained by contacting the publisher at laurensimonepubs@gmail.com.

Thank you for your support of the author's rights.

**Library of Congress Cataloging-in-Publication Data**
Lauren, Olivia and John, Melissa-Sue
Olivia Lauren's Guide to becoming an Actor/Olivia Lauren and Melissa-Sue John.
p. cm.
Illustration by Melissa-Sue John
Summary: A ten step guide for children interested in getting into the acting and modeling industry.
ISBN-13: 978-0-9979520-3-2
ISBN-10: 0997952032
BISAC: Juvenile Nonfiction / Careers
Title I. Series. Book 2.
1. Acting 2. Actor 3. Occupation 4. Jobs 5. Careers
2017900355

DEDICATION

*To Alkisha, Barbara, Dawn, Eric, Frances, Linda, and Patricia*

# CONTENTS

| | |
|---|---|
| Acknowledgment | i |
| Introduction | 1 |
| Chapter 1 | 3 |
| Chapter 2 | 4 |
| Chapter 3 | 5 |
| Chapter 4 | 6 |
| Chapter 5 | 8 |
| Chapter 6 | 10 |
| Chapter 7 | 14 |
| Chapter 8 | 15 |
| Chapter 9 | 16 |
| Chapter 10 | 20 |
| Conclusion | 22 |
| Glossary | 23 |
| About the Authors | 27 |
| Further Reading | 29 |

ACKNOWLEDGMENTS

We would like to thank Joseph Long, David Ramirez, Up on Sugar Hill Show for the use of the photos featured in this book.

We would also like to thank Alicia Angus, Paula Fraser, and Shay for feedback and proofreading.

# I AM OLIVIA LAUREN

I am an **actor**, model, and author.

I have been in TV shows, films, **musicals**, **commercials**, **public service announcements**, music videos, magazines, and fashion shows.

Photo Credit: Joseph Long

# DO YOU WANT TO BE AN ACTOR?

Before I even got to the stage or the TV screen, I had to complete a series of steps. Read the following chapters to learn 10 steps to guide you on your way to becoming an actor! The order of the steps may vary depending on your age, talent, and experience. But generally, all these steps must be taken.

Photo Credit: Joseph Long

# CHAPTER 1: TRUST FUND

Step 1: Open a Coogan Account.

The law protects children's future by putting away fifteen percent of the money they earn from performing into a trust fund called a Coogan Account. The remainder of the earnings is mailed to the performer. Go online or visit your local bank branch or credit union and set up your account. Learn how to balance how much you save and spend.

Photo Credit: Joseph Long

# CHAPTER 2: WORK PERMIT

Step 2: If you are a minor, apply for a child performer work permit.

In some states, child modeling, acting, or performing is regulated by labor laws. My parents completed the NY State Child Performer Permit application and submitted the application with a school form, a health form, and an official copy of the trust account.

Go online and search "Child performer work permit" with the state you will be working. Follow the instructions carefully and submit by mail.

# CHAPTER 3: PHOTOGRAPHS

Step 3: Get photographed and build your **portfolio**.

Snapshots are appropriate for babies, because they are constantly growing and changing. For older children, professional photos are recommended. It shows that you are serious about being an actor and also shows how versatile and photogenic you are. Find an experienced and affordable photographer. Take **headshots**, half- or three-quarter body, and full body portraits. Keep it simple: no hats or sunglasses to hide your face. Show different profiles of yourself smiling with and without showing your teeth.

Photo Credit: Joseph Long

# CHAPTER 4: REPRESENTATION

Step 4: Submit yourself to agencies for representation.

Make a list of trustworthy **talent agencies** and **management companies** in the city nearest you.

Legitimate companies have certain things in common. They do not ask for any money for fees, website maintenance, classes, or photographs. They are here to serve you. They make commission when you get a job. Legitimate companies do not pressure you into classes, photography sessions, or signing with them on the spot. Reputable companies do not advertise on the radio, in newspapers, or hang out in the mall or movie theaters. Finally, legitimate companies are knowledgeable about the market and do not make any promises for fame or success.

Once you have your list of credible companies, submit to each one online or by mail. Include three to four of the professional photos, a resume or cover letter that states your current age and date of birth, height, weight, clothes and shoe sizes, work experience, contact information, and **area of interest.** Within 3 weeks, you should receive a response, if they are interested. If not, resubmit in 6 months.

Photo Credit: @laurensimonepubs

# CHAPTER 5: PRACTICE

Step 5: Prepare to **audition**.

Find a **monologue** that you like. Study the monologue until you can say it from memory and with confidence.

Photo Credit: @laurensimonepubs

Get on camera experience. Start with a **slate** and create a **reel** by having your parent or a professional record your monologue.

Photo Credit: @laurensimonepubs

# CHAPTER 6: EXPERIENCE

Step 6: Practice your craft and get acting experience.

You can take classes or workshops to improve your performing skills, such as:
Acting for the camera
**Improvisation**
Performing arts
Voice lessons
**Voice over**

Photo Credit: @laurensimonepubs

Some classes are very costly. As an alternative, you can gain experience by volunteering to be in **student films.** Sign up with nearby film schools or performing centers. Student directors, student producers, and community theater are always looking for talent.

Photo Credit: David Ramirez

You can also sign up on online **casting sites** or **casting agencies** for background acting, theater, and other gigs. It is a good idea to be registered with the casting agencies that book jobs for the TV shows and films in that state.

Photo Credits: @laurensimonepubs

**Background acting** is a great place to meet other actors, directors, and producers. You will learn more about the acting industry, as well as the acting terminology, such as Rehearsal, Rolling, Lights, Camera, Action, Cut, and Reset.

Photo Credits: Joseph Long

# CHAPTER 7: AUDITION

Step 7: Go on auditions.

Diligently check and respond to your email, phone calls, and post mail. You could receive a message from a manager, an agent, or a casting director for an **audition** or **direct booking**. Be patient.

Unfortunately, **rejection** comes with the territory. The entertainment industry is very competitive. There are many actors trying out for the same opportunities. Some actors may be the same age, height, have a similar look or talent as you. However, remember there is only one you!

Do not quit if this is what you really want. Keep going on auditions.

# CHAPTER 8: THE CALL BACK

Step 8: Go to your **callback**.

When you least expect it, an agent, a manager, or a casting director will contact you for an audition, representation, or booking. Rehearse your lines, dress comfortably, and be on time. Always be professional, be yourself, and have fun.

Photo Credits: @laurensimonepubs

# CHAPTER 9: BOOKED

Step 9: Show up to your booking.

Once you are booked, you will receive a **call sheet** with your **call number**. The call sheet will tell you where and what time to show up. Alternatively, it may notify you the number to call or the webpage to go to access this information.

| Director: Ben Franklin<br>bfranklin@gmail.com<br>Producer: Natalia Perez<br>nperez@gmail.com | | Production:<br>**Discovered in NY** | Date:<br>June 4, 2016 | |
|---|---|---|---|---|
| Weather<br>Mostly Sunny<br>Sunrise: 5:26am<br>Sunset: 8:23pm | | CALL TIME<br>10:30am<br>9:45AM Pre-Call for production and camera | | |
| Location | Address | Parking | Notes | |
| 1. East River Park | East River Park New York, NY | Street Parking outside park | Entry points on Delancey St. and Houston St. | |
| Scene Description | Cast | Pages | D/N | Location |
| Scene 1/2<br>Olivia and Justice at the park | 1, 2, 3, BG | 1/8 | D | East River Park |
| Scene 2/2<br>Talent manager approaches Olivia and asks for her mom. | 1, 2,3,4,5 | 2/8 | D | East River Park |
| Number | Cast | Role | Call Time | Set Call |
| 1 | Olivia Lauren | Actor | 10:30am | 11:00am |
| 2 | Justice Lynn | Best friend | 10:30am | 11:00am |
| 3 | Alyssa Simone | Sister | 10:30am | 11:00am |
| 4 | Jennifer Brown | Talent manager | 10:30am | 11:00am |
| 5 | Linda Peters | Mother | 10:30am | 11:00am |

Photo Credit: @laurensimonepubs

Give yourself plenty of time to anticipate getting lost or dealing with traffic, parking, train or bus delays. Call and apologize if you are running late. When you arrive, you will check in with the production assistant. Have your **photo ID** and call number ready. You may be asked to sign a **talent release** and give photocopies of your work permit and trust fund. Always have plenty copies available and ensure none of your documents are expired.

Photo Credit: @laurensimonepubs

After completing your paper work, you will meet with **wardrobe** and the **hair and makeup** crew. Never show up empty handed. Always be prepared with your own clothing and makeup options. Make sure your hair, body, and clothes are clean and neat.

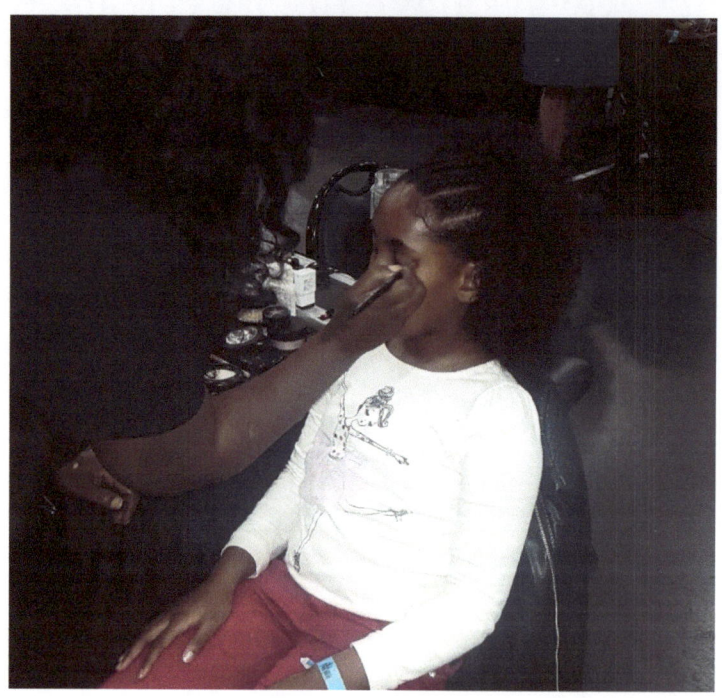

Photo Credit: @laurensimonepubs

Once your look is complete, you may have your photo taken.

Finally, you will be taken to set for rehearsal and begin filming. This is the moment you have been waiting for!

Photo Credits: @laurensimonepubs

# CHAPTER 10: CREDIT

Step 10: Add your **credits** to your resume.

As a **principal actor**, you may see your name in the credits at the beginning or the end of the production. As a background actor, your name may not be in the credits.

Photo Credit: @laurensimonepubs

Principal and supporting cast members' names appear on the internet movie database (IMDb). Search for yourself to see your list of credits. Keep your resume updated with all your work.

No matter what **role** you played or whether you received credit or not, you should always be proud of yourself. The production was completed with your participation.

Photo Credit: Up on Sugar Hill Show

# CONCLUSION

Congratulations! You have completed all ten steps. Celebrate each success, you deserve it. However, don't let it get to your head. Always be humble and grateful. It is now official. You are an actor, just like me!

Share your successes with your friends and family on social media. I would love to hear about your journey. Follow me on Instagram **@olivialaurenj** and tell me all about it.

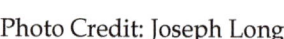

Photo Credit: Joseph Long

# GLOSSARY

**Actor:** a person who performs for the entertainment of others.

**Agent:** a person who applies for jobs for the actor.

**Areas of interest:** different parts of the entertainment industry including commercial, voiceover, theater, TV, or film.

**Audition:** an interview for actors.

**Background actor:** an extra or person with a nonspeaking role.

**Booked:** a confirmation that the actor was cast for a job.

**Call back:** a second audition.

**Call number:** the number on the call sheet next to your name.

**Call sheet:** a document that has the names, contact information, report location, and report times for all the cast and crew.

**Casting director:** a person who selects actors to play the various characters in a movie, TV show, or play.

**Cast member:** a principal or supporting actor in a production.

**Crew member:** a person involved in filming and producing the film or television show.

**Commercial:** a television or radio advertisement.

**Credits:** a list recognizing the participation of a person in a particular production, usually highlighting the production, the person's role, the director, production company, and crew.

**Direct booking:** getting a job based on your headshot or experience, without having to audition.

**Hair and makeup crew:** a team of professional hair stylists and makeup experts who provide hair styling and makeup for actors.

**Headshot:** a professional photograph that captures from the top of your head to your chest.

**Improvisation:** acting on the spot without preparation.

**Internet movie database (IMDb):** an online source that lists information on cast, production, crew, characters, plot, and reviews.

**Management company:** a company that provides a manager for the talent and works with many agencies to help develop the talent's career.

**Minor:** a person under the age of 18 years old that must be accompanied by an adult to work.

**Monologue:** a written text like a poem, commercial, or movie script.

**Music video:** a visual recording to a popular song.

**Musical:** a performance in a theater that includes speaking, singing, and dancing.

**Photo ID:** a document that identifies you by name and photograph such as a school ID, passport, or other government issued ID.

**Portfolio:** a book or folder of photographs and printed work.

**Principal actor:** an actor with a main role in a production.

**Public service announcement (PSA):** a message communicated through television or radio to a wide audience with the goal of raising awareness or changing attitudes or behavior.

**Reel:** a taped recording.

**Rejection:** not being chosen or selected after an audition or by an agency.

**Role:** the character played in a production.

**Set:** the place in which the production takes place.

**Script:** the written text of a TV show, movie, or other broadcast.

**Slate:** a paper or movie board used to identify the actor or production before filming.

**Student film:** a production directed and produced by college students for their class projects.

**Talent agency:** a company that provides the actor with an agent to help them get jobs.

**Trust fund:** a savings account for minors to access when they become an adult.

**Voice over:** the voice of a cartoon or the narrator of a commercial.

**Wardrobe crew:** members of the film crew who decide what each character should wear on set during the production.

**Work permit:** a legal document that informs the company hiring you that you have permission to work in that state.

# ABOUT THE AUTHORS

**Olivia Lauren** is a confident, funny, and hardworking child. She enjoys acting, modeling, reading, singing, dancing, yoga, and loves science, technology, engineering, and math (STEM). She has been featured in films, music videos ("My daughters living room" by Alge, "Polaridad" by Alex Ferreira, and "Stereotypes" by Black Violin), public service announcements, TV shows, theater, print magazines (Wild Child, AI Magazine, and the Big City Kids), and over a dozen runway shows. You can follow her at @olivialaurenj and https://www.facebook.com/olivialaurenj.

**Melissa-Sue John, Ph.D**. is passionate about teaching, scholarship, innovation, and mentorship. She is on a mission to increase literacy, STEM awareness, art appreciation, and diversity in children's literature. She is also a mom of two amazing children, wife to a great husband, evangelist, social psychologist, and travel enthusiast. You can follow her on Instagram at @laurensimonepubs.

# FURTHER READING

*Olivia Lauren's Occupations A to Z: A Children's Guide to Jobs and Careers* by Melissa-Sue John (Lauren Simone Publishing House).

www.ingramcontent.com/pod-product-compliance
Lightning Source LLC
LaVergne TN
LVHW071028070426
835507LV00002B/66